Cold Pasta Recipes That Everyone Will Love

Cold Pasta Cookbook for Quick and Easy Dishes

BY: Allie Allen

COOK & ENJOY

Copyright 2019 Allie Allen

Copyright Notes

This book is written as an informational tool. While the author has taken every precaution to ensure the accuracy of the information provided therein, the reader is warned that they assume all risk when following the content. The author will not be held responsible for any damages that may occur as a result of the readers' actions.

The author does not give permission to reproduce this book in any form, including but not limited to: print, social media posts, electronic copies or photocopies, unless permission is expressly given in writing.

My Gift to You for Buying My Book!

I would like to extend an exclusive offer to receive free and discounted eBooks every day! This special gift is my way of saying thanks. If you fill in the subscription box below you will begin to receive special offers directly to your email.

Not only that! You will also receive notifications letting you know when an offer will expire. You will never miss a chance to get a free book! Who wouldn't want that?

Fill in the subscriber information below and get started today!

https://allie-allen.getresponsepages.com/

Table of Contents

Easy and Delicious Cold Pasta Recipes 6

1) Oriental Cold Noodle Salad 7

2) Chicken Club Pasta Salad 9

3) Caesar Chicken Pasta Salad 11

4) Tomato and Gorgonzola Pasta Salad 13

5) Penne with Tomatoes and Green Beans 15

6) Pasta Salad with Salami and Mozzarella 17

7) Sweet Pea and Mint Pasta 19

8) Parmesan Pasta Salad 22

9) Orzo with Watermelon and Feta Cheese 24

10) Salmon Pasta Salad 27

11) Bacon and Avocado Pasta Salad 29

12) Kale Pasta Salad 32

13) Spaghetti Salad 34

14) Hawaiian Pasta Salad 36

15) Creamy Cheddar Pasta Salad 38

16) Fiesta Ranch Chicken Pasta Salad 40

17) BLT Pasta Salad 42

18) Mandarin Spinach Pasta Salad 44

19) Devilled Egg Pasta Salad 46

20) Mediterranean Pasta Salad 49

21) Broccoli Pasta Salad 52

22) Asparagus and Arugula Pasta Salad 54

23) Asian Pasta Salad 57

24) Strawberry Caprese Pasta Salad 59

25) Bacon Ranch Chicken Pasta Salad 61

About the Author 63

Author's Afterthoughts 65

Easy and Delicious Cold Pasta Recipes

sssssssssssssssssssssssssssssssssssssssssssssss

1) Oriental Cold Noodle Salad

This zesty cold salad has a Thai flavor and is great with chicken. Feel free to use spaghetti if you don't have soba noodles.

Yield: 8

Cooking Time: 1 hour 25 minutes

List of Ingredients:

- Soba noodles (15 oz., dried)
- Rice vinegar (1/3 cup)
- Lime juice
- Brown sugar (2 tbsp.)
- Red pepper flakes (2 tsp.)
- Peanuts (¼ cup, salted, chopped)
- Sesame oil (1 ½ tsp., dark)
- Soy sauce (1/3 cup)
- Lime zest
- Garlic (2 cloves, diced)
- Carrot (1 cup, shredded)
- Cilantro (½ cup, chopped)

sss

Methods:

1. Prepare noodles as directed on package including salt. Remove from heat, drain and run under cold water.

2. Put pasta in a large bowl along with all leftover ingredients. Toss to combine and put into refrigerator until chilled.

3. Serve and enjoy!

2) Chicken Club Pasta Salad

This delicious pasta salad can be eaten alone no need for anything but a fresh green salad to complement the mix. All the fillings from a club sandwich and topped with a creamy buttermilk dressing.

Yield: 4-6

Cooking Time: 15 minutes

List of Ingredients:

- Pasta (8 oz.)
- Chicken (2 cups, cooked and chopped)
- Tomato (1, seeds removed, chopped)
- Bacon (8 slices, cooked)
- Avocado (½, diced)
- Cheddar cheese (½ cup, cubed)

Dressing:

- Buttermilk (½ cup)
- Sour cream (½ cup)
- Fresh dill (1 tbsp.)
- Onion powder (1 tsp.)
- Black pepper
- Mayonnaise (½ cup0
- Chives (1 tbsp.)
- Parsley (1 tbsp.)
- Garlic powder (1 tsp.)
- Salt

sssssssssssssssssssssssssssssssssssssssssssssss

Methods:

1. Prepare dressing by putting all ingredients into a bowl and whisking to combine; refrigerate until needed.

2. Prepare pasta as directed on package including salt, remove from heat, drain, run under cold water and drain again. Put into a large bowl with dressing along with all remaining ingredient, toss to combine and chill.

3. Top with dressing, toss and serve. Enjoy!

3) Caesar Chicken Pasta Salad

The Caesar salad is an all-time favorite and when you add pasta to the already delicious mix you can share a more filling meal with your family. This pasta salad is bright and creamy and you will love every bite.

Yield: 10

Cooking Time: 1 hour 10 minutes

List of Ingredients:

- Penne pasta (1 lb.)
- Grape tomatoes (1 ½ cups)
- Parmesan cheese (½ cup, finely shredded)
- Chicken breasts (2, grilled and chopped)
- Romaine lettuce (6 leaves, sliced)
- Green onions (4, sliced)
- Black pepper (½ tsp.)
- Croutons (1 ½ cups)

Dressing:

- Mayonnaise (1 cup)
- Lemon juice (2 tbsp.)
- Worcestershire sauce (1 tsp.)
- Sour cream (1/3 cup)
- Garlic (1 clove, crushed)

sssssssssssssssssssssssssssssssssssssssssssssssss

Methods:

1. Prepare dressing by putting all ingredients into a bowl and whisking together.

2. Prepare pasta as directed on package including salt, remove from heat, drain, place in a large bowl and add half of dressing. Toss to combine and refrigerate until chilled.

3. Remove pasta from fridge and add leftover ingredients along with dressing and toss.

4. Serve and enjoy!

4) Tomato and Gorgonzola Pasta Salad

This salad is best if you use beef steak tomatoes because their juiciness add dimension to the dish however feel free to use smaller tomatoes. Top with your preferred crumbled cheese if you aren't for gorgonzola and enjoy.

Yield: 8

Cooking Time: 1 hour 10 minutes

List of Ingredients:

- Rigatoni pasta (16 oz.)
- Beefsteak tomatoes (1 ¼ lbs., seeds removed and chopped)
- Arugula (2 oz.)
- Gorgonzola cheese (4 oz., crumbled)

Vinaigrette

- Lemon juice (½ cup, fresh)
- Olive oil (1 cup)
- Honey (1 tbsp.)
- Black pepper
- Shallot (1, diced)
- Parsley (¼ cup, chopped)
- Dijon mustard (1 tbsp., whole grain)
- Salt

sssssssssssssssssssssssssssssssssssssssssssssssss

Methods:

1. Put all ingredients for vinaigrette in a bowl and use a whisk to mixture together; put aside until needed.

2. Prepare pasta as directed on package including salt, remove from heat, drain, place in a large bowl and add vinaigrette. Toss to combine and refrigerate until chilled.

3. Remove pasta from fridge and add cheese and tomatoes, toss and add pepper and salt.

4. Add arugula right before serving. Serve and enjoy!

5) Penne with Tomatoes and Green Beans

This simple pasta dish is tangy and comes to together in only a few minutes. The vinaigrette can be used in many other pasta salads and is truly bursting with flavor.

Yield: 8

Cooking Time: 35 minutes

List of Ingredients:

- Penne pasta (16 oz., whole wheat)
- Grape tomatoes (1 pint, cut in halves)
- Dill (¼ cup, chopped)
- Haricots verts (8 oz., sliced)

Vinaigrette:

- Lemon juice (½ cup, fresh)
- Olive oil (1 cup)
- Honey (1 tbsp.)
- Black pepper
- Shallot (1, diced)
- Parsley (¼ cup, chopped)
- Dijon mustard (1 tbsp., whole grain)
- Salt

sssssssssssssssssssssssssssssssssssssssssssssss

Methods:

1. Put all ingredients for vinaigrette in a bowl and use a whisk to mixture together; put aside until needed.

2. Prepare pasta as directed on package including salt, adding haricots in the final 2 minutes of cooking. Remove from heat, drain and run under cold water.

3. Put pasta in a large bowl along with vinaigrette and tomatoes. Toss to combine and put into refrigerator until chilled; add dill before serving.

6) Pasta Salad with Salami and Mozzarella

Sometimes you just need something light and simple. This parmesan pasta is just that; it is made from pasta, tomatoes, chives and parmesan.

Yield: 2

Cooking Time: 20 minutes

List of Ingredients:

- Gemelli (2 cups)
- Tomatoes (1 cup, cut in halves)
- Salami (2 oz., sliced)
- White wine vinegar (1 tbsp.)
- Black pepper
- Spinach (2 cups, chopped)
- Mozzarella (4 oz., cut up)
- Olive oil (3 tbsp.)
- Kosher salt

sssssssssssssssssssssssssssssssssssssssssssssssssss

Methods:

1. Prepare pasta as directed on package including salt. Remove from heat, drain and run under cold water.

2. Put pasta in a large bowl along with all leftover ingredients. Toss to combine and put into refrigerator until chilled.

3. Serve and enjoy!

7) Sweet Pea and Mint Pasta

This minty pasta and peas delight can be paired with grilled shrimp or other seafood for an elegant dinner. The torcetti pasta can be replaced with gemelli or cavatappi.

Yield: 10

Cooking Time: 30 minutes

List of Ingredients:

- Torcetti pasta (16 oz.)
- Green peas (1 cup)
- Sugar snap peas (1 lb.)
- Mint (1 cup, fresh and chopped)

<u>Vinaigrette</u>

- Lemon juice (½ cup, fresh)
- Olive oil (1 cup)
- Honey (1 tbsp.)
- Black pepper
- Shallot (1, diced)
- Parsley (¼ cup, chopped)
- Dijon mustard (1 tbsp., whole grain)
- Salt

sssssssssssssssssssssssssssssssssssssssssssssssss

Methods:

1. Put all ingredients for vinaigrette in a bowl and use a whisk to mixture together; put aside until needed.

2. Prepare pasta as directed on package including salt, adding snap peas in the final 2 minutes of cooking. Remove from heat, drain and run under cold water.

3. Put pasta and peas in a large bowl along with vinaigrette, mint and green peas. Toss to combine and put into refrigerator until chilled.

4. Serve and enjoy!

8) Parmesan Pasta Salad

Sometimes you just need something light and simple. This parmesan pasta is just that; it is made from pasta, tomatoes, chives and parmesan.

Yield: 4

Cooking Time: 20 minutes

List of Ingredients:

- Pasta (1 lb., shells)
- Parmesan (4 oz., crumbled)
- Chives (¼ cup, chopped)
- Tomatoes (2 pints, cut in halves)
- Olive oil (¼ cup, extra virgin)
- Kosher salt
- Black pepper

sssssssssssssssssssssssssssssssssssssssssssssss

Methods:

1. Prepare pasta as directed on package including salt. Remove from heat, drain and run under cold water.

2. Put pasta in a large bowl along with tomatoes, oil, salt, pepper, cheese and chives. Toss to combine and put into refrigerator until chilled.

3. Serve and enjoy!

9) Orzo with Watermelon and Feta Cheese

Orzo pasta may look like rice however it is not a grain; it just looks similar to it. Pairing orzo with creamy feta and juicy watermelon certainly makes for an interesting blend of flavors.

Yield: 6

Cooking Time: 3 hours 40 minutes

List of Ingredients:

- Orzo pasta (1 cup)
- Watercress/ baby arugula (4 cups)
- Watermelon (3 cups, seeds removed and chopped)
- Feta cheese (4 oz., crumbled)

Vinaigrette

- Lemon juice (½ cup, fresh)
- Olive oil (1 cup)
- Honey (1 tbsp.)
- Black pepper
- Shallot (1, diced)
- Parsley (¼ cup, chopped)
- Dijon mustard (1 tbsp., whole grain)
- Salt

sssssssssssssssssssssssssssssssssssssssssssssssss

Methods:

1. Put all ingredients for vinaigrette in a bowl and use a whisk to mixture together; put aside until needed.

2. Prepare pasta as directed on package including salt, remove from heat, drain, place in a large bowl and add vinaigrette. Toss to combine and refrigerate until chilled about 2-3 hours.

3. Remove pasta from fridge and add remaining ingredients, toss and add pepper and salt.

4. Serve and enjoy!

10) Salmon Pasta Salad

The salmon can be prepared in whatever way you prefer before adding it to this all in one meal. The tangy vinaigrette pairs with the fish perfectly.

Yield: 8

Cooking Time: 30 minutes

List of Ingredients:

- Rotini (8 oz.)
- Cucumber (1 cup, chopped)
- Mint (3 tbsp., fresh)
- Tomatoes (1 cup, halved)
- Salmon (12 oz., cooked)
- Red onion (¼ cup, chopped)

Vinaigrette

- Lemon juice (½ cup, fresh)
- Olive oil (1 cup)
- Honey (1 tbsp.)
- Black pepper
- Shallot (1, diced)
- Parsley (¼ cup, chopped)
- Dijon mustard (1 tbsp., whole grain)
- Salt

sssssssssssssssssssssssssssssssssssssssssssssssss

Methods:

1. Put all ingredients for vinaigrette in a bowl and use a whisk to mixture together; put aside until needed.

2. Prepare pasta as directed on package including salt. Remove from heat, drain and run under cold water.

3. Put pasta in a large bowl along with vinaigrette and tomatoes, cucumber, mint, salmon and onion. Toss to combine and put into refrigerator until chilled.

4. Serve and enjoy!

11) Bacon and Avocado Pasta Salad

This pasta salad is easy to make but the flavors that it is filled with are superb. Creamy avocado, salty bacon and herbed dressing blends together for a satisfying experience.

Yield: 4

Cooking Time: 20 minutes

List of Ingredients:

- Bacon (5 slices, chopped)
- Kosher salt
- Thyme (2 tsp.)
- Macaroni elbows (12 oz.)
- Avocados (2, seed and skin removed and chopped)
- Black pepper

Dressing:

- Mayonnaise (¾ cup)
- Lemon zest (1 ½ tbsp.)
- Thyme (1 tsp.)
- Olive oil (1/3 cup)
- Lemon juice (¼ cup, fresh)
- Sugar (1 tbsp.)
- Black pepper
- Kosher salt

sssssssssssssssssssssssssssssssssssssssssssss

Methods:

1. Put all ingredients for dressing in a bowl and use a whisk to mixture together; put in refrigerator until needed.

2. Prepare pasta as directed on package including salt, remove from heat, drain, place in a large bowl and put in refrigerator till needed.

3. Heat skillet and cook bacon until crisp, remove from pot and place on paper towels to remove excess oil.

4. Add bacon to pasta along with dressing, avocado, pepper and salt; toss to combine.

5. Serve and enjoy!

12) Kale Pasta Salad

If you prefer your pasta without the creamy texture then this kale concoction will be pleasing to you. The garlic infused oil and roasted pine nuts come together with kale for a simple yet flavor side.

Yield: 12

Cooking Time: 25 minutes

List of Ingredients:

- Bowtie pasta (1 lb.)
- Olive oil (¼ cup)
- Salt (½ tsp.)
- Kale (1 bunch, sliced)
- Balsamic vinegar (2 tbsp.)
- Pine nuts (3 tbsp.)
- Garlic (6 cloves)
- Black pepper (1 tsp.)
- Parmesan cheese (4 oz., shaved)

sssssssssssssssssssssssssssssssssssssssssssssss

Methods:

1. Prepare pasta as directed on package including salt, remove from heat, drain, run under cold water and drain again. Put into a large bowl and put aside till needed.

2. Heat oil in skillet and cook garlic for about 5-7 minutes until golden, stirring frequently. Add pepper and salt and remove from pot and pour over pasta.

3. Put kale in skillet and sauté for 4-5 minutes until wilted then add to pasta then add pine nuts to skillet and roast for 3-5 minutes then add to pasta.

4. Stir mixture to combine then add cheese and vinegar and toss.

5. Chill, serve and enjoy!

13) Spaghetti Salad

Spaghetti is usually used in hot dishes however it is great in this cold salad. It is flavorful as well as can feed a large unit.

Yield: 15

Cooking Time: 28 minutes

List of Ingredients:

- Spaghetti (1 lb., broken)
- Zucchini (1, chopped)
- Green pepper (1, diced)
- Red Onion (1, chopped)
- Canned olives (4.5 oz., drained and sliced)
- Tomatoes (3, diced)
- Zucchini squash (1 yellow, diced)
- Red pepper (1, diced)
- Cucumber (1, diced)
- Cheddar cheese (8 oz., cubed)

Dressing:

- Italian dressing (16 oz.)
- Paprika (1 tsp.)
- Parmesan cheese (¼ cup, grated)
- Garlic powder (¼ tsp.)

ssssssssssssssssssssssssssssssssssssssssssssssss

Methods:

1. Put all ingredients for dressing in a bowl and use a whisk to mixture together; put in refrigerator until needed.

2. Prepare pasta as directed on package including salt, remove from heat, drain, place in a large bowl and put in refrigerator till needed.

3. Add dressing to spaghetti along with tomatoes, peppers, cucumber, zucchini, onion and squash; toss to combine.

4. Serve and enjoy!

14) Hawaiian Pasta Salad

Get the tastes of the tropics with this Hawaiian inspired dish. This one the kids will definitely love with ham and bits of pineapple-yum!

Yield: 8

Cooking Time: 23 minutes

List of Ingredients:

- Pasta (8 oz.)
- Red pepper (1, diced)
- Green onion (1, sliced thin)
- Pineapple tidbits (14 oz.)
- Ham (2 cups, chopped)

Dressing:

- Mayonnaise (½ cup)
- Dijon mustard (1 tbsp.)
- Honey (1 tsp.)
- Black pepper
- Sour cream (¼ cup)
- Pineapple juice (1/3 cup)
- Garlic powder (¼ tsp.)

sssssssssssssssssssssssssssssssssssssssssssssssss

Methods:

1. Prepare dressing by putting all ingredients into a bowl and whisking to combine; refrigerate until needed.

2. Prepare pasta as directed on package including salt, remove from heat, drain, run under cold water and drain again. Put into a large bowl with dressing along with all remaining ingredient, toss to combine and chill.

3. Top with dressing, toss and serve. Enjoy!

15) Creamy Cheddar Pasta Salad

This pasta salad is vibrant from rich cheddar cheese and the herbed dressing. With every taste you will love it more and more.

Yield: 6

Cooking Time: 20 minutes

List of Ingredients:

- Rotini pasta (1 lb.)
- Celery (3 ribs, diced)
- Onion (¼ cup, diced)
- Bell pepper (1 red, minced)
- Cheddar cheese (8 oz., cubed)

Dressing:

- Mayonnaise (1 cup)
- Apple cider vinegar (2 tbsp.)
- Parsley (½ tsp.)
- Sugar (¼ cup)
- Black pepper (½ tsp.)

sssssssssssssssssssssssssssssssssssssssssssssss

Methods:

1. Put all ingredients for dressing in a bowl and use a whisk to mixture together; put in refrigerator until needed.

2. Prepare pasta as directed on package including salt, remove from heat, drain, place in a large bowl and put in refrigerator till needed.

3. Add dressing to pasta along with bell pepper, onion, cheese and celery.

4. Serve and enjoy!

16) Fiesta Ranch Chicken Pasta Salad

This Mexican inspired dish is chock full of beans, olives, cheese and all the goodies that are associated with Mexican cuisine.

Yield: 6-8

Cooking Time: 15 minutes

List of Ingredients:

- Pasta (16 oz.)
- Taco mix (1 pack)
- Canned kidney beans (8 oz., drained and rinsed)
- Onion (1, chopped)
- Canned olives (8 oz., sliced)
- Tomatoes (2, chopped)
- Chicken breasts (1 ½ lbs., cooked and chopped)
- Canned black beans (8 oz.)
- Frozen corn (8 oz.)
- Green pepper (1, chopped)
- Cheddar cheese (2 cups, grated)

Dressing:

- Mayonnaise (2 cups)
- Fiesta dip mix (1 pack)
- Buttermilk (1 cup)

sssssssssssssssssssssssssssssssssssssssssssssss

Methods:

1. Prepare dressing by putting all ingredients into a bowl and whisking to combine; refrigerate until needed.

2. Prepare pasta as directed on package including salt, remove from heat, drain, run under cold water and drain again. Put into a large bowl along with all remaining ingredient, toss to combine and chill.

3. Top with dressing, toss and serve. Enjoy! (can be topped with chips before serving)

17) BLT Pasta Salad

Are you a lover of the BLT sandwich then try this pasta salad that was inspired by it. This salad is both appealing to the eyes and the palate. The best thing it is ready in only 20 minutes because you will be using items you probably already have.

Yield: 6

Cooking Time: 20 minutes

List of Ingredients:

- Bow tie pasta (1 lb.)
- Bacon (1 lb.)
- Red onion (1, diced)
- Tomatoes (2, chopped)
- Romaine lettuce (10 leaves, chopped)
- Pepper
- Salt

Dressing:

- Italian dressing (1 cup)
- Ranch dressing (½ cup)

sssssssssssssssssssssssssssssssssssssssssssssss

Methods:

1. Put all ingredients for dressing in a bowl and use a whisk to mixture together; put in refrigerator until needed.

2. Prepare pasta as directed on package including salt, remove from heat, drain, place in a large bowl and put in refrigerator till needed.

3. Heat skillet and cook bacon until crisp. Remove from heat and place on paper towels to remove excess oil; chop and put aside.

4. Add dressing to pasta along with lettuce, onion, bacon and tomatoes; add pepper and salt to taste and toss to combine.

5. Serve and enjoy!

18) Mandarin Spinach Pasta Salad

This Asian inspired pasta dish is refreshing and healthy and is a mixture of sweet and tangy that is delicious. The vinaigrette is simply too good.

Yield: 4

Cooking Time: 15 minutes

List of Ingredients:

- Bowtie pasta (8 oz.)
- Craisins (½ cup)
- Canned mandarin (4 oz., drained)
- Spinach (4 cups)
- Cilantro (¼ cup, chopped)
- Cashews (1/3 cup)

Dressing:

- Rice wine vinegar (1/3 cup)
- Onion powder (½ tsp.)
- Black pepper (¼ tsp.)
- Olive oil (½ cup)
- Teriyaki sauce (1/3 cup)
- Garlic powder (½ tsp.)
- Salt (¼ tsp.)
- Sugar (1 tbsp.)

sssssssssssssssssssssssssssssssssssssssssssssss

Methods:

1. Prepare dressing by putting all ingredients into a bowl and whisking to combine; refrigerate until needed.

2. Prepare pasta as directed on package including salt, remove from heat, drain, run under cold water and drain again. Put into a large bowl along with spinach, nuts, cilantro, craisins and mandarin; toss to combine and chill.

3. Top with dressing, toss and serve. Enjoy!

19) Devilled Egg Pasta Salad

Who doesn't love devilled eggs? Now you can combine two of your faves to make a delectable dish that you can show off at the next potluck or picnic.

Yield: 8

Cooking Time: 20 minutes

List of Ingredients:

- Macaroni elbow (1 lb.)
- Eggs (6, hard boiled)
- Paprika

Dressing:

- Mayonnaise (2 cups)
- Pickle brine (2 tbsp.)
- Celery (3 ribs, diced)
- Sweet relish (1/3 cup)
- Mustard (4 tbsp.)
- Red onion (½, diced)
- Sea salt
- Pepper

sssssssssssssssssssssssssssssssssssssssssssssss

Methods:

1. Put all ingredients for dressing in a bowl and stir to mix together; put in refrigerator until needed.

2. Prepare pasta as directed on package including salt, remove from heat, drain, place in a large bowl and put in refrigerator till needed.

3. Take shells off eggs and dice; put aside until needed.

4. Add dressing to pasta and toss to combine then add eggs and fold. Top with paprika.

5. Serve and enjoy!

20) Mediterranean Pasta Salad

Fresh herbs are what bring this Greek inspired salad to life. The vibrant dressing will have you clearing your dish in no time. If you don't have fresh herbs use half the amount of dried.

Yield: 8

Cooking Time: 40 minutes

List of Ingredients:

- Garlic (2 tbsp.)
- Kosher salt (1 tsp.)
- Lemon juice (½ tsp., fresh)
- Lemon zest
- Grape tomatoes (½ cup, halved)
- Basil (2 tbsp., fresh, chopped)
- Bell pepper (1 cup, green, diced)
- Feta cheese (8 oz.)
- Olive oil (¼ cup, extra-virgin)
- Oregano (2 tbsp., fresh)
- Black pepper (½ tsp.)
- Pasta (12 oz.)
- Kalamata olives (½ cup, sliced)
- Mint (1 tbsp., fresh, chopped)
- Red onion (½ cup, chopped)
- Canned artichoke hearts (14 oz., sliced with stems)

sssssssssssssssssssssssssssssssssssssssssssssss

Methods:

1. Heat oil in a skillet and sauté garlic and oregano with salt and pepper for 8 minutes until garlic is golden. Take from heat and add lemon juice; put aside till needed.

2. Prepare pasta as directed on package including salt, remove from heat, drain and put into a large bowl along with lemon juice mix. Toss to combine and put aside for 5 minutes.

3. Add leftover ingredients to pasta except cheese. Toss again to combine and refrigerate until chilled then add cheese.

4. Serve and enjoy!

21) Broccoli Pasta Salad

This pasta salad pulls together in little or no time. The crunchy broccoli goes well with the creamy cheese dressing; top with cranberries for a hint of tart.

Yield: 8

Cooking Time: 20 minutes

List of Ingredients:

- Bow tie pasta (1 lb.)
- Broccoli (1 head)
- Almonds (silvered)
- Cranberries (1/3 cup, dried)
- Bell peppers

Dressing:

- Ranch dressing (1 cup, three-cheese blend)
- Salt
- Pepper

sssssssssssssssssssssssssssssssssssssssssssssssssss

Methods:

1. Put all ingredients for dressing in a bowl and stir to mix together; put in refrigerator until needed.

2. Prepare pasta as directed on package including salt, add broccoli in final 2 minutes, remove from heat, drain, place in a large bowl and put in refrigerator till needed.

3. Add dressing to pasta and broccoli toss to combine then add bell peppers, almond and cranberries; toss to combine.

4. Serve and enjoy!

22) Asparagus and Arugula Pasta Salad

This bright green salad is way to get those important greens in. This will be a crowd pleaser and can be paired with just about any meat.

Yield: 8

Cooking Time: 20 minutes

List of Ingredients:

- Pasta (1 lb., whole wheat)
- Lemon juice (3 tbsp.)
- Red wine vinegar (1 tbsp.)
- Goat cheese (2/3 cup, crumbled)
- Black pepper
- Asparagus (1 lb., trimmed and cut into bite size pieces)
- Lemon zest (1 tbsp.)
- Olive oil (1 tbsp.)
- Baby arugula (2 cups)
- Basil (¼ cup)
- Pine nuts (¼ cup, optional)

sssssssssssssssssssssssssssssssssssssssssssss

Methods:

1. Prepare pasta as directed on package including salt, add asparagus in final 3 minutes remove from heat, drain, run under cold water and drain again.

2. Put pasta in a bowl and add zest, oil, vinegar and lemon juice; toss to combine then add cheese, pepper, arugula, pine nuts (optional) and basil. Toss again to combine and refrigerate until chilled.

3. Serve and enjoy!

23) Asian Pasta Salad

This refreshing pasta dish is filled with so many flavors that your taste buds will simply go crazy. Juicy mangoes with creamy avocado and red cabbage topped with an insatiable sesame vinaigrette.

Yield: 4

Cooking Time: 25 minutes

List of Ingredients:

- Macaroni elbows (8 oz.)
- Mango (1, peel removed and chopped)
- Red cabbage (¼ cup, shredded)
- Pine nuts (2 tbsp.)
- Black pepper
- Avocado (1, diced)
- Carrot (1, shredded)
- Green onion (1, sliced)
- Kosher salt

Dressing:

- Sesame oil (2 tsp.)
- Sesame seeds (½ tsp.)
- Sesame oil (2 tsp.)
- Sugar (1 ½ tsp.)

sssssssssssssssssssssssssssssssssssssssssssssss

Methods:

1. Put all ingredients for dressing in a bowl and whisk to mix together; put in refrigerator until needed.

2. Prepare pasta as directed on package including salt, remove from heat, drain, place in a large bowl and put in refrigerator till needed.

3. Add avocado, carrot, green onion, salt, mango, cabbage, pine nuts and pepper to pasta and toss. Top with dressing and toss.

4. Serve and enjoy!

24) Strawberry Caprese Pasta Salad

Who says all pasta dishes have to be made with mayo? How about a sweet, dessert-like pasta dish that everyone will love? No mayo needed here just five ingredients that will make this pasta salad irresistible.

Yield: 10

Cooking Time: 1 hour 10 minutes

List of Ingredients:

- Pasta
- Mozzarella (fresh, diced)
- Balsamic glaze (4 tbsp.)
- Strawberries (1 pint, pitted and sliced in halves)
- Basil (½ cup, chopped)
- Chocolate syrup (for topping)

sssssssssssssssssssssssssssssssssssssssssssssss

Methods:

1. Prepare pasta as directed on package including salt, remove from heat, drain, run under cold water and drain again. Put into a large bowl along with ½ of glaze and chill.

2. Remove pasta from fridge and add leftover ingredients except syrup and toss.

3. Serve and enjoy!

25) Bacon Ranch Chicken Pasta Salad

You can use whatever style of chicken to like to change up the taste of this pasta dish. This is a quick go-to meal if you have leftover chicken.

Yield: 8

Cooking Time: 20 minutes

List of Ingredients:

- Pasta (2 cups)
- Frozen peas (1 cup)
- Bacon (6 slices, chopped)
- Black pepper
- Chicken (2 cups, cooked and shredded)
- Tomatoes (1 cup, chopped)

Dressing:

- Ranch dressing (½ cup)

ssssssssssssssssssssssssssssssssssssssssssssssss

Methods:

1. Prepare pasta as directed on package including salt, add peas in final 5 minutes, remove from heat, drain, place in a large bowl and add dressing. Toss to combine and refrigerate until chilled.

2. Heat skillet and cook bacon until crispy, remove and put on paper towels to remove excess oil.

3. Remove pasta from fridge and add chicken, tomatoes, bacon and pepper.

4. Serve and enjoy!

About the Author

Allie Allen developed her passion for the culinary arts at the tender age of five when she would help her mother cook for their large family of 8. Even back then, her family knew this would be more than a hobby for the young Allie and when she graduated from high school, she applied to cooking school in London. It had always been a dream of the young chef to study with some of Europe's best and she made it happen by attending the Chef Academy of London.

After graduation, Allie decided to bring her skills back to North America and open up her own restaurant. After 10 successful years as head chef and owner, she decided to sell her business and pursue other career avenues. This monumental decision led Allie to her true calling, teaching. She also started to write e-books for her students to study at home for practice. She is now the proud author of several e-books and gives private and semi-private cooking lessons to a range of students at all levels of experience.

Stay tuned for more from this dynamic chef and teacher when she releases more informative e-books on cooking and baking in the near future. Her work is infused with stores and anecdotes you will love!

Author's Afterthoughts

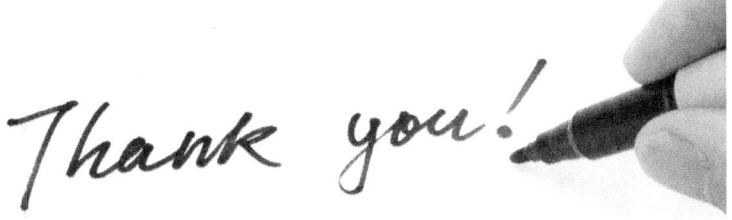

I can't tell you how grateful I am that you decided to read my book. My most heartfelt thanks that you took time out of your life to choose my work and I hope you find benefit within these pages.

There are so many books available today that offer similar content so that makes it even more humbling that you decided to buying mine.

Tell me what you thought! I am eager to hear your opinion and ideas on what you read as are others who are looking for a good book to buy. Leave a review on Amazon.com so others can benefit from your wisdom!

With much thanks,

Allie Allen

Printed in Great Britain
by Amazon